Introduction

Guitar from the Beginning is designed for beginner guitarists who have no previous knowledge of music or musical notation.

Ideally any student learning to play a musical instrument should have a teacher, especially in the early stages. However, the desire to play the guitar is spreading so rapidly that the supply of teachers invariably does not meet the demand. This series is designed to meet the needs of both the student lucky enough to find a teacher (and, incidentally, for the teachers themselves, whether working in schools, colleges, evening classes or privately) and also the determined and enthusiastic pupil who wants to teach himself.

Learning to play a musical instrument takes time. Patience is essential and the pupil should take care to master each stage thoroughly before attempting the next.

New notes are introduced in boxes:

New points of musical notation are introduced in clouds:

All cloud contents should be understood before attempting the music which follows. Boxes and clouds are easily spotted when looking back through the book for revision.

Book 1 covers notes up to the third fret on all six strings. Playing position and right and left hand techniques are described in detail. The emphasis throughout is on achieving a good, productive technique, and at the same time becoming musically literate.

The guitar is treated both as a solo instrument and also as an accompanying instrument. Solo playing helps to build a sound classical technique, while the ability to sing and play at the same time is not only a good exercise in musicianship, but is also considered by many to be a real social asset!

During lessons and practice periods the student is strongly advised to:

★ **Check the playing position regularly, and correct if necessary;**

★ **Listen to the sounds being produced, and improve them if possible;**

★ **Play everything slowly and evenly at first. Speeding on the guitar as on the roads, usually leads to disaster.**

Contents

Look at Your Guitar

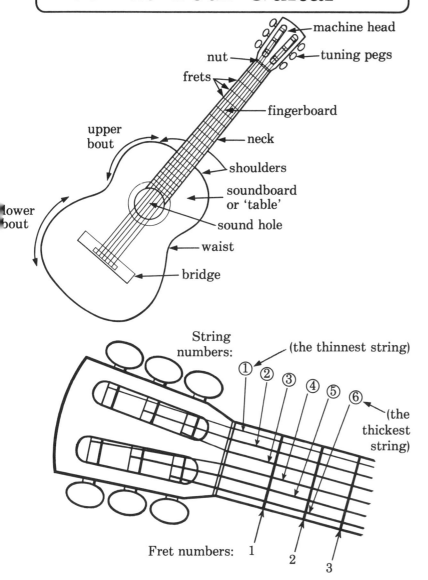

machine head

nut

tuning pegs

frets

fingerboard

upper bout

neck

shoulders

soundboard or 'table'

lower bout

sound hole

waist

bridge

String numbers:

(the thinnest string)

① ② ③ ④ ⑤ ⑥

(the thickest string)

Fret numbers: 1 2 3

Get to know your instrument, and the names of its various parts.

Three Rules for String Players

*The THINNER the string, the HIGHER the sound;
*The TIGHTER the string, the HIGHER the sound;
*The SHORTER the string, the HIGHER the sound.

The thinner the string, the higher the sound. Look at the six strings of your guitar. They get thicker as you go to the left. Play the strings in turn and you will find the first rule is true. Remember this rule when fitting new strings.

The tighter the string, the higher the sound. Pluck the thinnest string and listen to the sound. Gently turn the tuning peg to which it is attached. The string will either tighten or slacken. Turn the peg the other way. Now, plucking the string all the time, turn the peg slightly each way in turn. You will find the second rule is true. Remember this rule when tuning the guitar.

The shorter the string, the higher the sound. Play string ①, the thinnest string. Now put a left-hand finger on the string just behind one of the FRETS, so that the string is held firmly over the fret. You have shortened the string, which can now vibrate only between the fingered fret and the BRIDGE. Play the string again. You will find the third rule is true.
Remember this rule when using the fingerboard.

Understanding and Learning to Read Music

Music is a language, and can be written down and read like other languages.

Musical notes have letter-names. The English alphabet has 26 letters, but the musical alphabet has only 7 — A, B, C, D, E, F and G.

Music is written on a STAVE (a set of five lines).

A stave must have a CLEF (a French word, meaning 'key') at the beginning of it. The clef 'unlocks' the stave by telling us that the notes written on it are of high or low pitch. It also tells what their letter-names will be.

Guitar music uses the TREBLE CLEF —
The treble clef tells us that the music will be fairly high, and that, reading from the bottom of the stave, the notes written on the LINES will be E, G, B, D and F; and the notes written in the SPACES will be F, A, C and E.

As notes go HIGHER up the stave, they go FORWARD in the musical alphabet.

As notes go LOWER down the stave, they go BACKWARDS in the musical alphabet.

The stave is not big enough for the top and bottom notes on the guitar, and we use LEGER LINES. These are extra lines, above and below the stave.

This is the lowest note on the guitar.

You will probably be surprised to discover that the notes you play on the guitar will not sound the same as the notes you read on the stave.

If you read and play this note A it will actually sound as this note A

The distance, or INTERVAL, between these two sounds is called on OCTAVE. An octave is a distance of EIGHT notes, including both the first and last notes. Notes one octave apart have a similar sound, and the same letter-name.

Why not write down the real notes?
The range of guitar notes is fairly low. To write them at their true pitch we would need another stave with the BASS CLEF to start with, going into a stave with the treble clef for the higher notes.

If we transpose the notes up one octave we need only one stave, using leger lines for the highest and lowest notes.

Do not tune the strings to the notes actually written. They must sound one octave lower.

Tuning the Guitar

These are the six strings of the guitar, from the thickest to the thinnest:

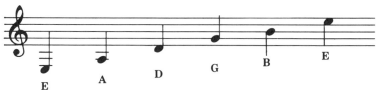

Play the thickest string, string ⑥. This should sound low note E.

Check this note either using a set of guitar pitch-pipes or by playing the note on the piano (remembering that it will be one octave lower than the written note).
If the string is out of tune, correct it by either tightening or slackening the string using the tuning peg, playing the string frequently until the sound is right.

String ⑤ should sound note A:

The interval between this note and the E of string ⑥ is a 4th (a distance of 4 notes, including both the first and last notes).

Think of the first two notes of the tune 'Away in a Manger'. These two notes are a 4th apart. Tune your string ⑤ until the two notes E and A sound just like the beginning of the tune.

As a check, put a left hand finger just behind fret 5 on string ⑥. This will give you note A to check with string ⑤.

Between strings ⑤ and ④, and between ④ and ③, the interval is also a 4th. So you can use the same tune to help you judge the interval correctly. You can also check with fret 5 on the adjacent lower string.

The interval between strings ③ and ② is only a 3rd.

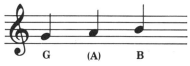

The first two notes of 'While Shepherds Watched' will help you to hear this interval. To check it, use the 4th fret on string ③.

Between strings ② and ① the interval is again a 4th, so think 'Away in a Manger' again, and use fret 5 on string ② to check.
Always check the tuning before you start to play. It does not matter at this stage how you sound the strings. The tuning checks can be done with the guitar lying flat on the table, and you can use your right hand thumb or a finger to play the string. What does matter is that you listen very carefully, and learn to know when the sound is right and when it is wrong.

The Playing Position
and how to use the right hand

Sit on an ordinary chair with your left foot on a footstool. Place the guitar over your left thigh as shown in the diagram. If possible, check by looking at yourself in a full-length mirror. Since no two guitar players are exactly alike physically, try to find an experienced player or teacher to check your position at this stage. (Bad habits are easy to acquire and difficult to cure.)

Both hands are going to work very hard. The playing position must help them to work efficiently and yet stay relaxed.

First practise the right-hand position away from the guitar.

Position the book on the table in front of you, so that with your forearm and hand resting on the table and your elbow just off the edge of the table, your thumb tip touches the line arrowed. Now move your hand forward and curve the finger joints until the index, middle and ring finger tips are standing along the line. The finger joints (not the tips) will be pushed a little over the line. The little finger is too short and not used, so let it relax and then forget about it.

Now, keeping the thumb and three fingers on the line, pivot the forearm on the edge of the table, and lift the wrist off the table. This will make a gentle curve from fingertips to elbow, with the arm balanced and supported by the table edge.

1. Correct hand position seen from side.

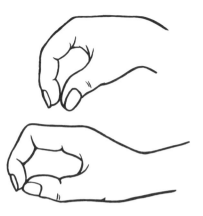

2. Incorrect position seen from side, with fingers, wrist and forearm producing an 'S' bend rather than one curve.

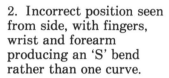

With your hand in the correct position raise and lower each finger in turn. Make sure each finger returns to the line.

In guitar music, each right hand finger has a letter name. The letter name is the first letter of the Spanish name for each finger or thumb.

p —pulgar (thumb)
ι —indice (index finger)
m—medio (middle finger)
a —anular (ring finger)

Practise raising and lowering in this order:

p ι m a a m ι p

Now imagine that the line is an itch and scratch it with each finger in turn:

p ι m a

Pretend that each finger is a horse's hoof and paw with each one in turn:

p ι m a
a m ι p

Now repeat all three stages: raising and lowering, scratching and pawing with your hand raised about one centimeter above the page. Try to make your fingers land on the line from a short distance away. Balance your arm on the table edge to help you hold the position comfortably.

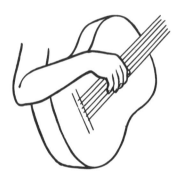

Now try it on a guitar string!

Sit comfortably, with the guitar at the correct angle over your left thigh. Pivot the right forearm over the edge of the lower bout of the guitar. The finger tips should be over the strings, near to the sound hole. Line up the thumb and finger tips along string ①. Practise raising and lowering thumb and finger tips on the string. The scratching and pawing should be done with the hand held OFF the strings.

Playing the Open Strings
Right hand Apoyando

Apoyando is a Spanish word. It is a way of playing the strings with the right hand to give a firm, clear sound.

Rest your thumb on string ⑥, the thickest string. Keep it straight, but relaxed. Check your right hand position—the arm pivoting on the lower bout of the guitar, and a curve from finger tips through the wrist to the elbow. Play string ① with the index finger *i* using the 'pawing' action, but aim the finger towards the next string so that it comes to rest touching string ②. When you move your finger away from string ② you might hear a slight sound, but do not worry at this stage. It will help if you try not to push too hard into string ② before making the next stroke.

This is the note you are playing—note E.

A number in a circle shows which string to play:

① ② ③ ④ ⑤ ⑥

Small letters show which right-hand finger to use:

p—thumb, *i*—index, m—middle, a—ring finger

o means 'NO LEFT-HAND FINGERS' or 'OPEN STRING'.

This note is a crotchet. ♩ or ♪ Crotchets are walking-pace notes, not too fast or slow. Tap some even beats on the table top. Imagine they are footsteps walking along. This is the speed at which to play crotchets.

Play this steadily and evenly with your index finger:

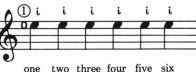

Apoyando

Count: one two three four five six

Now use the right-hand middle finger:

Apoyando

Count: one two three four five six

Now, still using the apoyando stroke, use index and middle fingers in turn:

Apoyando

Count: one two three four five six

Try the same exercise starting with the middle finger:

m   *i*   m   *i*   m   *i*
Count: one two three four five six

It does not matter which finger you start with when playing apoyando, but you must alternate the fingers. Never repeat a finger, or your playing will become uneven.

8

Rhythm and Counting

Play these 6 crotchets on string ① – note E.

LOUD Soft LOUD Soft LOUD Soft

Can you hear how the notes, although evenly spaced, seem to be grouped in twos?

You can feel and hear the grouping clearly if you emphasise the first note of each group. When music is written down, the groups are shown by BAR LINES.

Play the following, and make the first note in each bar slightly stronger than the others. Count out loud as you play. Do not stop at the bar lines.

Count: ONE two three four   ONE two three four

Count: ONE two three ONE two three ONE two three

Count: ONE two   ONE two

Bars and bar lines

A bar line is written before the first note of each group, i.e. the 'strong' one. The lines divide the music into BARS. Each bar has an equal number of counts – usually 2, 3 or 4. The crotchet ♩ is worth one count, or BEAT.

LOUD Soft LOUD Soft LOUD Soft LOUD Soft

A piece of music always ends with a DOUBLE BAR LINE, just as a sentence always ends with a full stop.

The time signature

At the beginning of every piece of music, just after the clef, you will find two numbers:

$\frac{2}{4}$ $\frac{3}{4}$ $\frac{4}{4}$

The top number tells you how many beats you must count in each bar. The bottom number tells you how much each beat is worth.

$\frac{2}{4}$ tells you to count in twos, and that each count will be worth a crotchet. (We sometimes call a crotchet a quarter note.)

Think of your counts as BEATS – for $\frac{2}{4}$ count two 'walking-pace' beats in every bar.

9

Open string ② note B

B

This note is produced on string ② without any left-hand fingers on. (OPEN STRING)

1. Four beats in a bar:

Count:

Remember to emphasise the first note of each bar.

2. Three beats in a bar:

Sing or say: B B B   E E E   B B B   E B E

3. Two beats in a bar:

Sing or say: E E   B B   B B   E E

Open string ③ note G

G

(String ③ open)

♩ This sort of note is a MINIM. It is twice as long as a crotchet. Count two full beats on this note before moving on to the next.

Play these tunes, which use the three notes you now know. Watch out for minims.

Sing or say: G G G G   B B B B

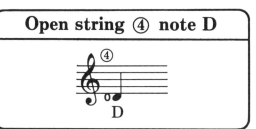

Open string ④ note D

1. Play:

Lazy Days

Wagon Train

Tap some beats with your foot.
Clap the beats at the same time with your hands.

tap	tap	tap	tap
clap	clap	clap	clap

Both your feet and hands are playing crotchets.

Now keep your foot tapping crotchets evenly and clap twice as fast with your hands:

tap	tap	tap	tap
clap clap	clap clap	clap clap	clap clap

You are dividing each beat into two. These half-beat notes are quavers.

QUAVERS are quick notes. Quavers are twice as fast as crotchets.
Two quavers make one beat.

One quaver on its own looks like this: ♪

Two quavers look like this: ♪♪

But they can also be joined together to look like this:

11

Play this:

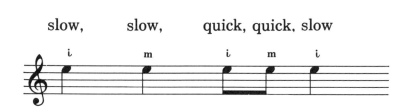

slow,   slow,   quick, quick, slow

Try this same rhythm on string ②, then ③, then ④.

If ♩=1 beat and ♫=1 beat, how many beats are there in the following? Tap them on the table top, counting the beats as you play.

Now play the following tunes.

Come to the Cookhouse Door

Count: ONE   two and three   four   ONE (two) three (four)

April Showers

Ding Dong Bell

March Winds

How to Use the Left Hand

Bring your left hand up in front of your face, with the palm towards you. Stretch the fingers outwards and upwards, then bend every finger joint so that the nails are facing you. Keep the thumb relaxed all the time. Imagine that you are holding on to a horizontal rod, with your fingers curving round it.

Now slide the book in between your finger tips and thumb so that the line (again representing a string) comes under the finger tips. The thumb will probably be in a position similar to this:

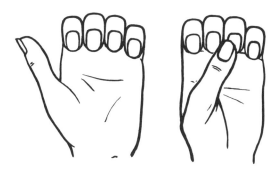

Left hand position

It naturally stays straight, pointing out away from the hand. Keeping it straight, pivot it forward from the base joint (where it joins the hand) so that it comes under the book, and under the fingers. Now stretch the fingers out along the line. See how far you can reach, keeping them all in contact with the line. Do this every day, and try to stretch a little bit further each time.

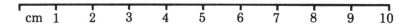

Left-hand fingers are indicated by numbers:

Left hand fingering

Using the printed line, position your left hand fingers along it and try to raise and lower each finger in turn (keeping the others down).

1 1 2 2 3 3 4 4

Now try it in this order:

1 2 3 4 3 2 1

Now transfer to the guitar.

Imagine that string ① is the line printed at the top of the page. Bring the hand up and curve the fingers over to land on string ① so that the first finger is just behind fret 1.

You now have frets to measure the length of your stretch, rather than centimeters. At first your four fingers will be fairly closely bunched together along the string. Your constant aim will be to stretch out until, keeping finger 1 down behind fret 1, you can place finger 2 behind fret 2, finger 3 behind fret 3 and finger 4 behind fret 4. This may seem impossible at first. You may need to move the hand up a little to reach frets 3 and 4. But remember that this is what you will be aiming to do when your hand is fully developed.

Numbers: Strings, Fingers and Frets

A number in a circle tells you on which string to play. A small number near a note tells you which left hand finger to use. For the time being this small number will also show which fret to use.

This is your first 'fingered' note on the guitar:

Note A

The numbers tell you that it is played on string ③, with the left hand finger 2 placed behind fret 2.

Play:

A A A A

Practise:

Say:

G A G A G G - A A B B A A

Seconds Away!

You have learned these notes:

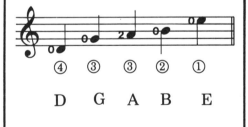

④ ③ ③ ② ①

D G A B E

Play them, and then read from right to left and play them backwards!

Lullaby

Close your eyes and go to sleep, Angels sweet watch will keep.

Soon you'll be in slumber deep; Sleep, sleep, go to sleep.

When you know this tune quite well, try singing the words as well as playing the tune on the guitar.

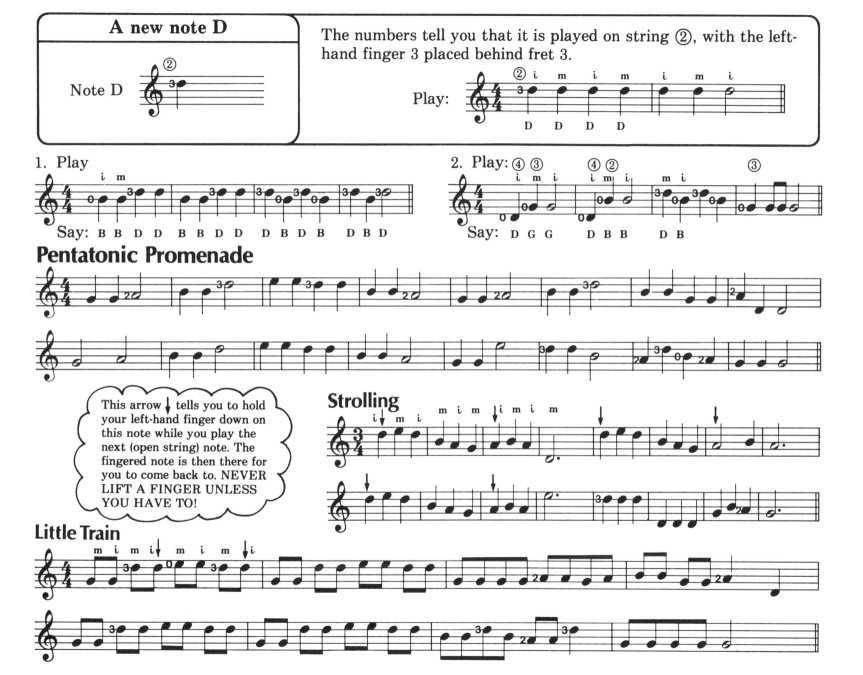

A new note D

Note D ② 3

The numbers tell you that it is played on string ②, with the left-hand finger 3 placed behind fret 3.

Play: ② i m i m i m i
D D D D

1. Play
i m
Say: B B D D B B D D D B D B D B D

2. Play: ④ ③ ④ ② ③
i m i i m i i m i
Say: D G G D B B D B

Pentatonic Promenade

This arrow ↓ tells you to hold your left-hand finger down on this note while you play the next (open string) note. The fingered note is then there for you to come back to. NEVER LIFT A FINGER UNLESS YOU HAVE TO!

Strolling

i m i m i m i m i m

Little Train

m i m i i m i m i

A la Claire Fontaine

A   la   clai——re   fon-tai-ne,   M'en   al-lant   pro-me-ner,   Je   trou-vais   l'eau si bel-le

Que   je m'y   suis bai-gné.   Il   y a long- temps que je t'ai-me, Ja-   mais je ne t'ou-bli-er-ai.

Haggis Hop

Now you know all of these notes:

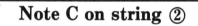

Note C on string ②

Note C

String ②, fret 1, finger 1

Practise:

1.

2.

This is a CROTCHET REST. When you see it count one beat but do not play a note. It means SILENCE for one beat.

Practise:

16

Au Clair de la Lune

Farewell to Summer

Practice Makes Perfect

Anacrusis

The next tune starts like this:
An incomplete bar at the beginning of a tune is called an ANACRUSIS. The music does not start on a strong beat, but on a weak one.

The bar line shows clearly where the first strong beat is, and the anacrusis leads up to it. Notice that the last bar of all has only 3 beats. Add this to the anacrusis and you have the number of beats in a bar shown by the time signature—4.

The Old Man in the Wood

Count: 4   1 2 3 4   1 (2) 3 4

1 (2) (3)

London's Burning

Count: 3 and 1   2   3 and 1   2

Playing Notes Together: Your First Chords

Right hand Tirando

When you want to play two or more strings at the same time you cannot use apoyando, because when your finger comes to rest on the next string it prevents it from vibrating. You must therefore strike the strings with your fingers in the same way as you did when playing apoyando, but aiming to miss the next string instead of coming to rest on it. This method of playing is indicated by the Spanish word TIRANDO. Make the strings vibrate across the guitar rather than 'up and down'. If you pluck strings upwards you will get an ugly sound.

Place your index finger tip on string ③.
Place your middle finger tip on string ②.
These are the two fingers you will use to sound G and B together.

Notes written above each other are played together and called chords.

How to use the right hand thumb

Replace i and m on strings ③ and ② respectively. Place your thumb (p) on string ④.
Thumb and fingers work in opposite directions, so make sure the thumb is not behind the fingers, but out a little way along the string. Keeping i and m in position, practise moving the thumb with a circular motion, pivoting from its base joint. Keep it straight. Bring it up and back towards you, then down and across the string it is

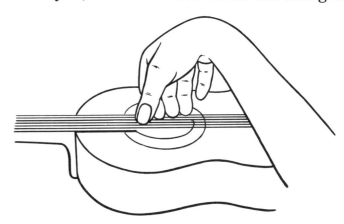

going to play. Follow through, bringing it back up and over, ready to start a new stroke. Then try to do it without any support from i and m.

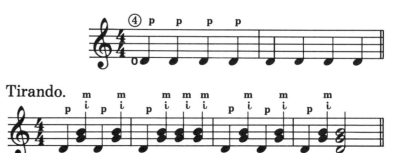

Bass note G (or low G)

Bass note G

String ⑥, finger 3, fret 3

It is so low that it needs two leger lines below the stave.

Chord G

Repeat marks

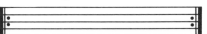

Everything in between these special bar lines is repeated.

In exercises 2 and 3 move the thumb freely between the bass notes G and D, keeping the hand as still and relaxed as possible.

Practise splitting the G chord into 'ums' and 'chas'. Notice the repeat marks. Play the whole thing twice through. Tirando.

In exercises 4, 5 and 6 the notes of the chord are played separately. Keep the left hand third finger down on low G for the whole excercise:

Ten in the Bed

Play the tune first and get to know it well. Then play the chords and sing the tune.

There were ten in the bed and the little one said, 'Roll

over! Roll over!' So they all rolled over and one fell out. *There were

*Repeat from 10 down to 1, finishing the last verse here.

Brother Joseph

You already know this tune. Sing the top line and play the chords.

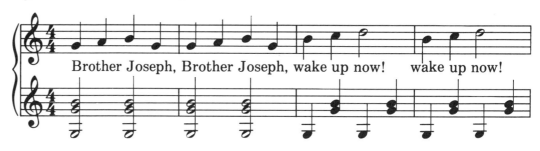

Brother Joseph, Brother Joseph, wake up now! wake up now!

Ring the bell for matins, ring the bell for matins, ding ding dong, ding ding dong.

Exercise

Chord D7

Before actually playing this chord, practise placing and lifting the left-hand fingers 1 and 2 on strings ② and ③ until they go down together on notes C and A.

Play: *Tirando*

Practise: *Tirando*

Whole bar rest or four-beat rest

A~Hunting We Will Go

Andante by Carulli

Variation on the Andante

21

Dotted Minim

This note is worth three beats.
(A dot makes a note half as long again.)

I Saw Three Ships

I saw three ships come sail-ing in On Christ-mas Day, On Christ-mas Day. I

saw three ships come sail——ing in On Christ-mas Day in the morn——ing.

Two new notes on string ①

F G

The Bouncing Ball

Switchback Ride

Now the Day is Over

22

Tirando practice on the top three strings

You have not yet used the right-hand ring finger. It is a naturally weak finger and you will need to persevere to make it just as efficient as *i* and *m*. Two alternative right-hand fingerings are given in the first two exercises. Practice the top one first, then the lower one.

March

In this piece you will be playing two things at once—a tune and an accompaniment.

The tune is played with the right-hand thumb throughout. The notes of the accompaniment are played with middle and index fingers. The tune notes have their tails going down and the accompaniment notes have their tails going up. Let the long tune notes ring on under the accompaniment notes. Try to hear the two parts working together.

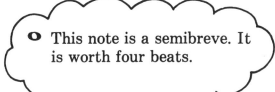

𝅝 This note is a semibreve. It is worth four beats.

Tirando

Two new notes on string ④

E F

Practise:

Ah! Poor Bird

Ah! Poor bird! Take thy flight Far above the sor-rows of this sad night.

Hide and Seek

Wellington Waltz

(An "Um cha cha" dance. The Waltz became very popular during the 19th century, especially in Vienna.)

Here again you have a tune and accompaniment to play together. Let the tune notes sound clearly, and play the accompaniment lightly.

D.C. al Fine
(Italian—Da Capo al Fine)
Go back to the beginning and play through again until the word 'FINE'—then stop.

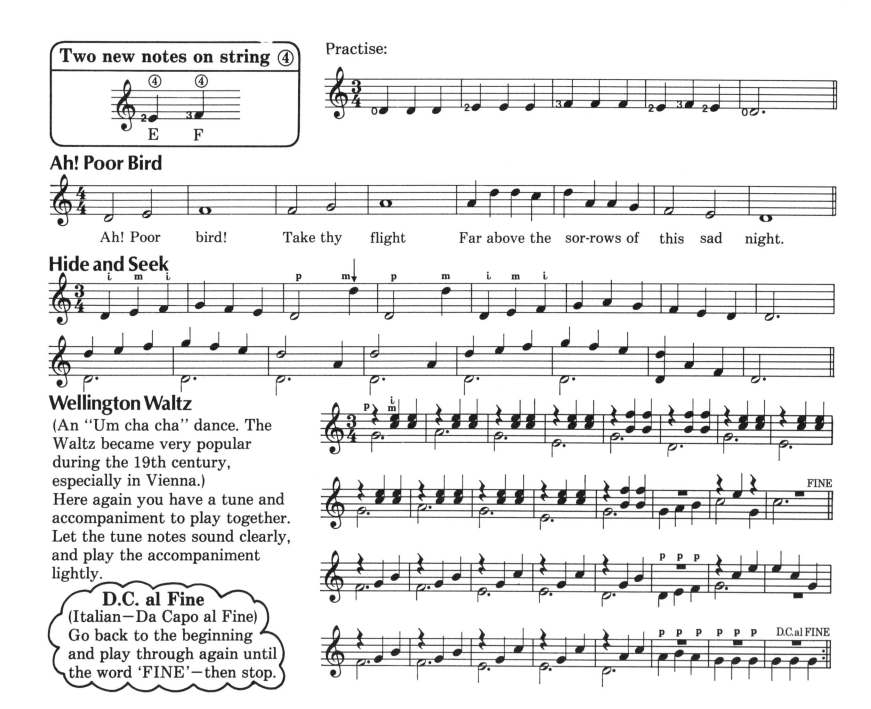

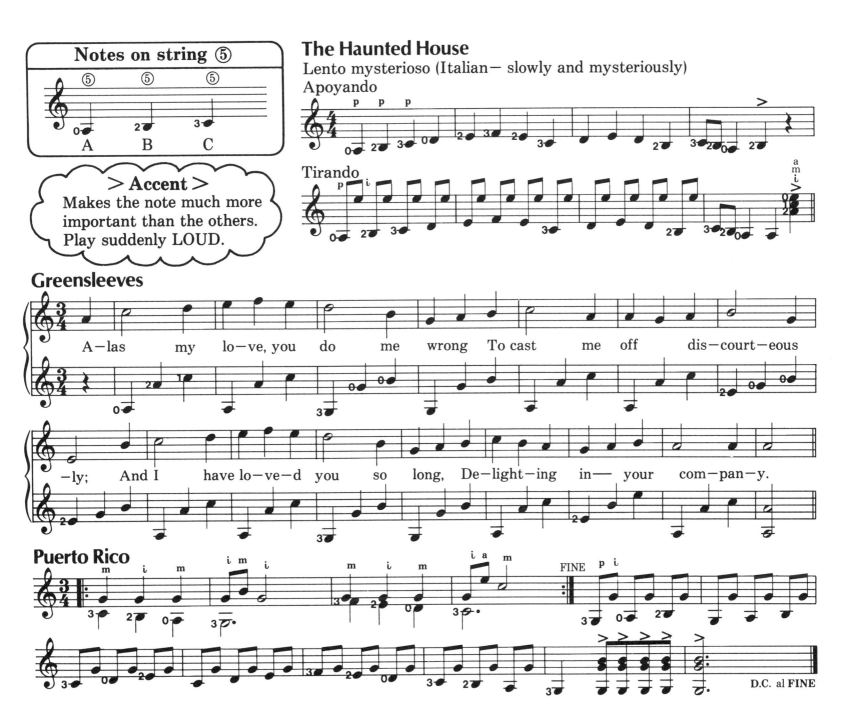

The Scale of C Major

Play any open string. Then play again, but with the first finger at the first fret. The interval between these two sounds is called a semitone. It is the smallest interval you can play on the guitar, because each fret is 'one semitone away' from the next.

Now play the open string, miss one fret and play with your 2nd finger at the 2nd fret. You have played an interval called a tone. The major scale is a succession of eight notes using intervals of tones and semitones in a special order. Here is an ascending major scale. Notice how each half of the scale follows the same pattern.

Try using different fingerings, e.g. m i m i etc

m a m a etc

a m a m etc

Now try it the other way round and without any fingering to help you:

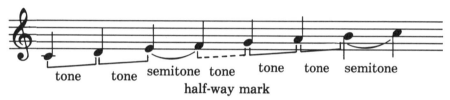

The scale of C major starts and ends on C.

Swingboats

Cresta Run

Two chords in the key of C

Chord C Practise:

Chord G7 Practise:

Skip to my Lou

Lou,   Lou,   skip to my Lou,   Lou,   Lou,   skip to my Lou.

Lou,   Lou,   skip to my Lou,   skip to my Lou, my dar———ling

Waltz by Carulli

One Man Went to Mow

Make up your own accompaniment to this song. Use the chords indicated. The magic word is 'meadow'. Whenever this word is sung, the chord changes. Try it in key C first:

Now try it in key G, using chords G and D7. Play string ② open. This is your starting note for singing:

Play string ① open. This is your starting note for singing. (Four beats in a bar)

C		C	C		G7

One man went to mow, went to mow a meadow

G7		G7	G7		C

One man and his dog went to mow a meadow

G		G	G		D7

One man went to mow, went to mow a meadow

D7		D7	D7		G

One man and his dog went to mow a meadow

Buffalo Gals

Sing:

Buffa—lo gals, won't you come out tonight, come out tonight, come out tonight?

Play:

Buffalo gals, won't you come out tonight And dance by the light of the moon?

Hush, Little Baby

Hush, little baby, don't say a word; Mama's gonna buy you a mocking bird.

28

Notes on string ⑥

You already know this G:

Here are two more notes on this string:

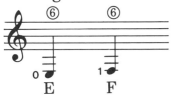

Troubadour

These scale exercises will help to improve the performance of each hand and also to give you plenty of practice with reading the notes you have learned so far.

Play all the exercises apoyando. Try different fingerings, e.g.

i m i m etc
m i m i
m a m a
a m a m
p p p p

Exercise 1

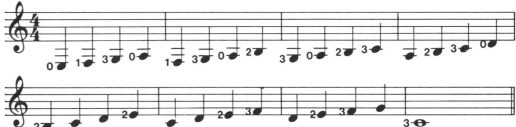

Variations

a

b

29

Try to make your own variations on Exercise 2.

Exercise 2

Sentimental Serenade

Notice that the 4th finger occasionally plays at the 3rd fret. This is because either the 3rd finger is occupied at the 3rd fret on a lower string, or it helps to avoid a nasty left-hand stretch.

Fandango

Some of the low melody notes have accents on them. This tells you to play them with a little more force, so that they stand out. Be careful not to strike too hard on the thick bass strings, or you will make an unpleasant buzzing sound.

Down in the Valley

This song accompaniment uses chords C and G7, decorated with note A on the second beat.
Practise holding down left-hand fingers 1 and 3 on either chord, and placing and releasing finger 2 on note A (string 3).

1. Down in   the   va———————lley,   va—lley   be—low,————————————

Hang your head   o——————ver,   hear   the   wind   blow.————————————

2. Hear the wind blow, love, hear the wind blow.
   Hang your head over, hear the wind blow.

Prairie Lullaby

Indian Brave

8/98 (31549)